BIGGEST HITS of 95-96

Project Manager: Carol Cuellar

CONTENTS

ONE OF US

Words and Music by
ERIC BAZILIAN
Arranged by DAN COATES

God had a name, ___ what would it be and would you call it to his face,
God had a face, ___ what would it look like and would you want to see,

THE MOST BEAUTIFUL GIRL IN THE WORLD

Composed by ☥

Arranged by DAN COATES

10

MENTAL PICTURE

Words and Music by
JON SECADA and
MIGUEL A. MOREJON
Arranged by DAN COATES

12

Verse 2:
Time was of the essence,
And as usual the day turns into minutes.
Sharing love and tenderness,
That's the nerve you struck in me that sent a signal.
To the other side,
(Girl, I don't know)
Saying my blind side.
And if a ... *(To Chorus:)*

ALWAYS AND FOREVER

Words and Music by
ROD TEMPERTON
Arranged by DAN COATES

Slowly ♩. = 50

(with pedal)

1. Al - ways and for - ev - er,____ each mo - ment with you
2. There'll al - ways be sun - shine____ when I look at you.

is just like a dream to me that some - how came true.
Some - thing I can't ex - plain, just the things that you do.

And I know to - mor - row____ will still be the same,
And if you get lone - ly, ____ call me and take

Always and Forever - 3 - 1

ANGEL EYES

Composed by
JIM BRICKMAN
Arranged by DAN COATES

Angel Eyes - 3 - 1

Angel Eyes - 3 - 3

ANGELS AMONG US

Words and Music by
BECKY HOBBS and DON GOODMAN
Arranged by DAN COATES

Additional lyrics

Spoken: *When life held troubled times and had me down on my knees*
There's always been someone to come along and comfort me.
A kind word from a stranger, to lend a helping hand,
A phone call from a friend just to say I understand.
Sung: *Now, ain't it kind of funny, at the dark end of the road,*
Someone lights the way with just a single ray of hope.
(To Chorus)

BECAUSE YOU LOVED ME
(Theme from "UP CLOSE & PERSONAL")

Words and Music by
DIANE WARREN
Arrnaged by DAN COATES

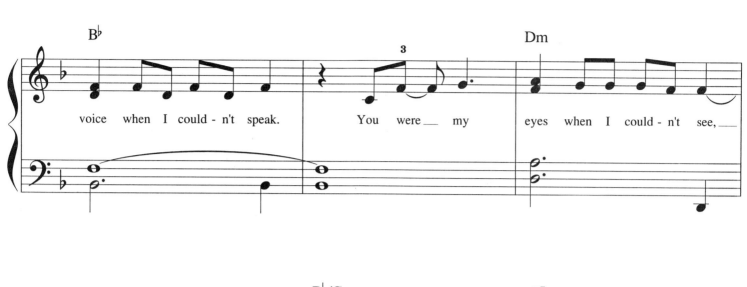

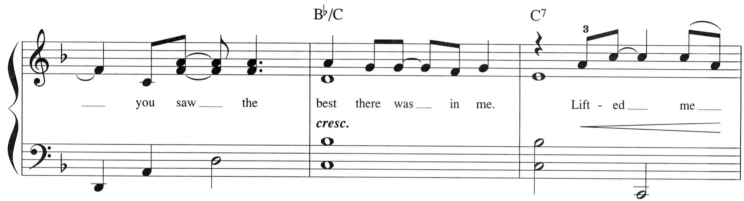

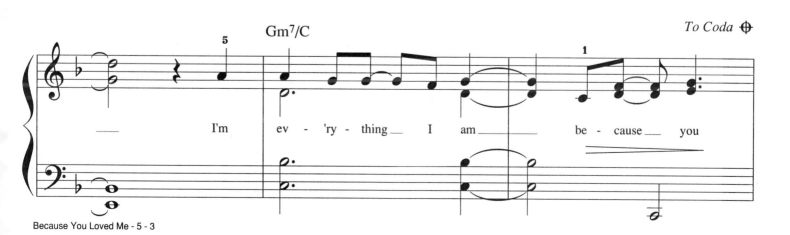

Because You Loved Me - 5 - 3

COME TO MY WINDOW

Lyrics and Music by
MELISSA ETHERIDGE
Arranged by DAN COATES

Moderately slow ♩ = 76

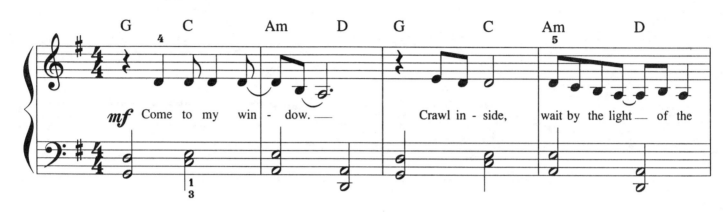

Come to my win - dow. ___ Crawl in - side, wait by the light ___ of the

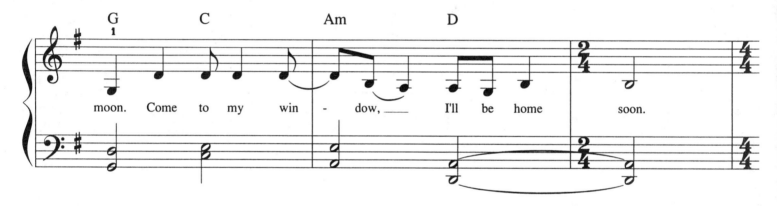

moon. Come to my win - dow, ___ I'll be home soon.

Faster ♩ = 92

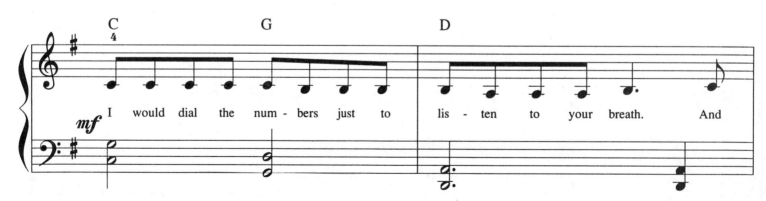

I would dial the num - bers just to lis - ten to your breath. And

Come to My Window - 4 - 1

Verse 2:
Keeping my eyes open, I cannot afford to sleep.
Giving away promises I know that I can't keep.
Nothing fills the blackness that has seeped into my chest.
I need you in my blood, I am forsaking all the rest.
Just to reach you,
Just to reach you.
Oh, to reach you.   *(To Chorus:)*

THE DAY I FALL IN LOVE
(Love Theme from "Beethoven's 2nd")

Words and Music by
CAROLE BAYER SAGER, CLIF MAGNESS
and JAMES INGRAM
Arranged by DAN COATES

The Day I Fall in Love - 5 - 1

DON'T TURN AROUND

Words and Music by
DIANE WARREN and
ALBERT HAMMOND
Arranged by DAN COATES

DREAMING OF YOU

Words and Music by
TOM SNOW and
FRAN GOLDE
Arranged by DAN COATES

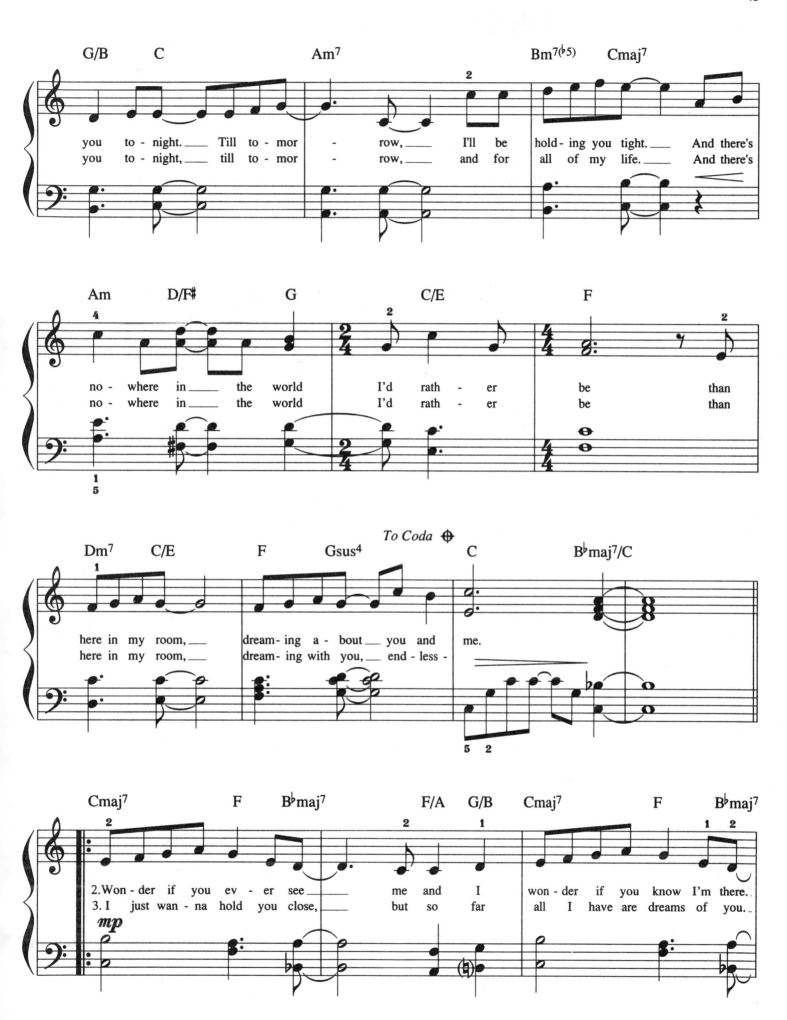

44

from WAITING TO EXHALE

EXHALE
(Shoop Shoop)

Words and Music by
BABYFACE
Arranged by DAN COATES

FOR YOUR LOVE

Music and Lyrics by
STEVIE WONDER
Arranged by DAN COATES

For Your Love - 3 - 2

52

For Your Love - 3 - 3

IF YOU GO

Words and Music by
JON SECADA and MIGUEL A. MOREJON
Arranged by DAN COATES

Verse 2:
Sorry if you felt misled
But I know what I feel, I know what I said, baby.
God, I hope you believe, believe in all that we can be,
The future in us together in love.
You're the reason I'm strong.
Don't you think I don't know
This is where I belong?
Give me the time to say that you're mine
To say that you're mine.
(To Chorus:)

From the Original Motion Picture Soundtrack "DON JUAN DeMARCO"

HAVE YOU EVER REALLY LOVED A WOMAN?

Lyrics by
BRYAN ADAMS and ROBERT JOHN "MUTT" LANGE

Music by
MICHAEL KAMEN
Arranged by DAN COATES

Have You Ever Really Loved a Woman? - 4 - 1

HOLD ME, THRILL ME, KISS ME

Words and Music by
HARRY NOBLE
Arranged by DAN COATES

HOUSE OF LOVE

Words and Music by
GREG BARNHILL, KENNY GREENBERG
and WALLY WILSON
Arranged by DAN COATES

Moderate rock beat

House of Love - 4 - 1

Verse:

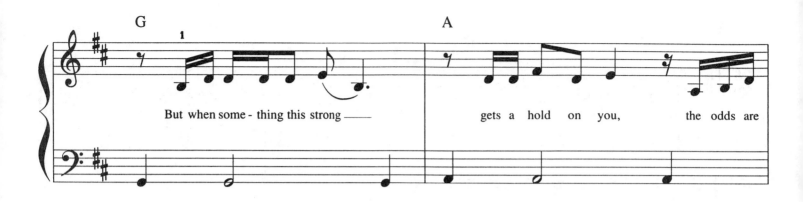

But when some-thing this strong ___ gets a hold on you, the odds are

nine-ty nine to one it's got a hold on ___ him, too. ___ Well, I

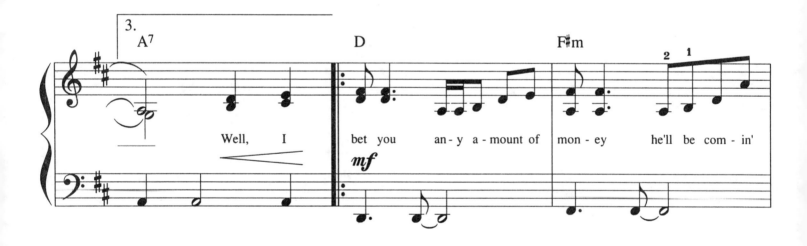

Well, I bet you an-y a-mount of mon-ey he'll be com-in'

back to you. ___ Ooh, I know there ain't no doubt a-bout it, some-times life is

Verse 2:
Now, when the house is dark and you're all alone inside,
You've gotta listen to your heart, put away your foolish pride.
Though the storm is breakin' and thunder shakes the walls,
There with a firm foundation ain't it never, never, never gonna fall.
(To Chorus:)

Verse 3:
Though the storm is breakin' and thunder shakes the walls,
There with a firm foundation ain't it never, never, never gonna fall.
(To Chorus:)

I CAN LOVE YOU LIKE THAT

Words and Music by
STEVE DIAMOND, MARIBETH DERRY
and JENNIFER KIMBALL
Arranged by DAN COATES

I Can Love You Like That - 4 - 1

IN THIS LIFE

Words and Music by
MIKE REID and ALLEN SHAMBLIN
Arranged by DAN COATES

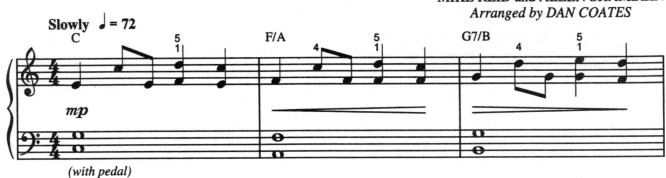

For all I'd been blessed with in my life,

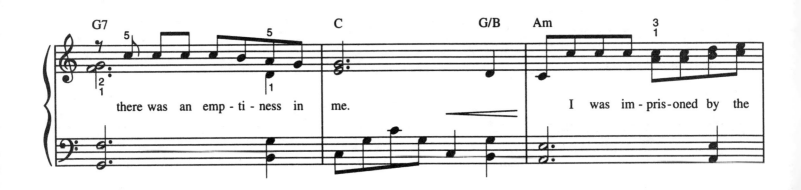

there was an emp-ti-ness in me. I was im-pris-oned by the

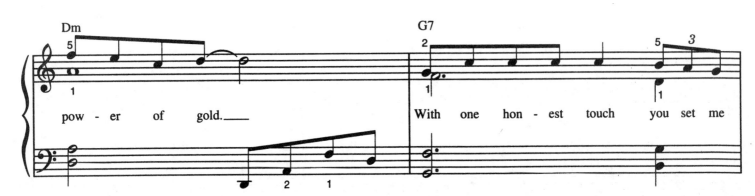

pow - er of gold.___ With one hon-est touch you set me

In This Life - 3 - 1

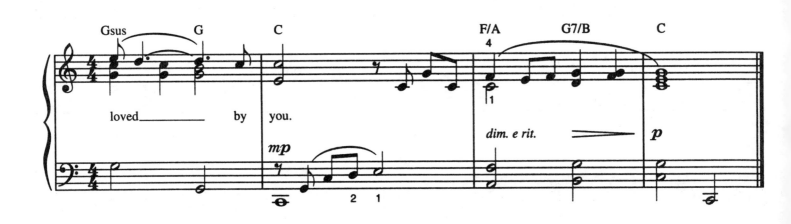

Verse 2:
For every mountain I have climbed,
Every raging river crossed,
You were the treasure that I longed to find.
Without your love I would be lost.
(To Chorus:)

I'D LIE FOR YOU
(AND THAT'S THE TRUTH)

Words and Music by
DIANNE WARREN
Arranged by DAN COATES

Moderately slow ♩ = 88

1. I'd nev-er tell you one lie,___ I'd nev-er let you down. I'd nev-er leave, I'd be the
2. Just take a look in my eyes,___ you'll see a love that's blind. Just take a hold of my hand,

I'd Lie for You - 5 - 1

I'LL BE THERE FOR YOU
(Theme from "FRIENDS")

Words by
DAVID CRANE, MARTA KAUFFMAN, ALLEE WILLIS,
PHIL SOLEM and DANNY WILDE

Music by
MICHAEL SKLOFF
Arranged by DAN COATES

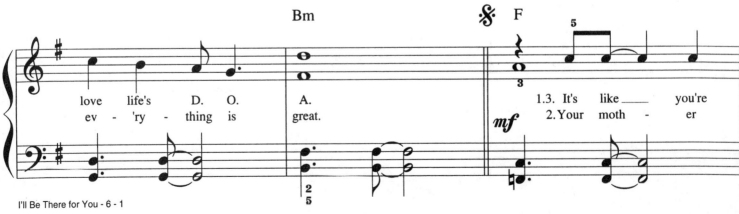

I'll Be There for You - 6 - 1

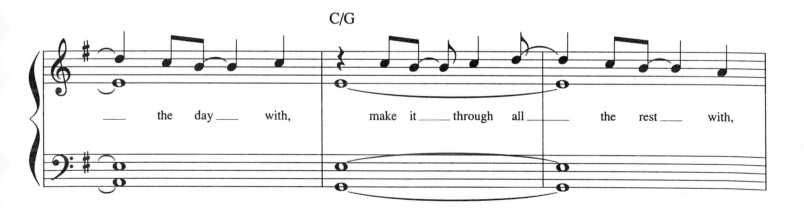

Theme from the Motion Picture "WITH HONORS"

I'LL REMEMBER

Words and Music by
**PATRICK LEONARD,
MADONNA CICCONE** and
RICHARD PAGE
Arranged by DAN COATES

Moderately slow

Say good-bye___ to not know-ing when___ the
In - side___ I was a child___ that

truth and my___ whole life___ be - gan.___ Say good-bye___ to
could not mend___ a bro - ken wing.___ Out - side___ I

not know-ing how___ to cry, you taught___ me that.
looked for a way___ to teach my heart___ to sing. And I'll re-

I'll Remember - 4 - 4

THE KEEPER OF THE STARS

Words and Music by
KAREN STALEY, DANNY MAYO and DICKEY LEE
Arranged by DAN COATES

The Keeper of the Stars - 4 - 1

LEAVE VIRGINIA ALONE

Words and Music by
TOM PETTY
Arranged by DAN COATES

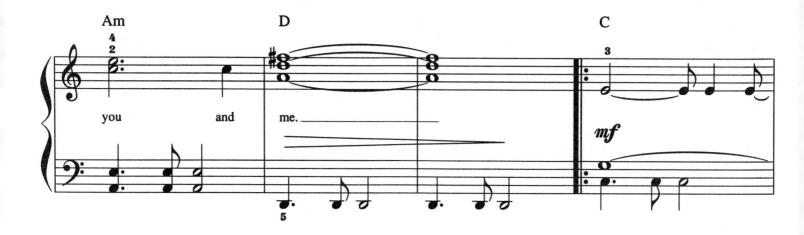

you and me.

Verse 2:
You should have seen her back in the city,
Poetry and jewels, broke all the rules.
She was as high as a Georgia pine tree,
Make-up and pills, overdue bills. So... *(Chorus)*

Verse 3:
She's a loser, she's a forgiver.
She still finds good, where no one could.
You ought to want her more than money,
Cadillacs and rust, emeralds and dust. So... *(Chorus)*

OPEN ARMS

Words and Music by
STEVE PERRY and
JOHNATHAN CAIN
Arranged by DAN COATES

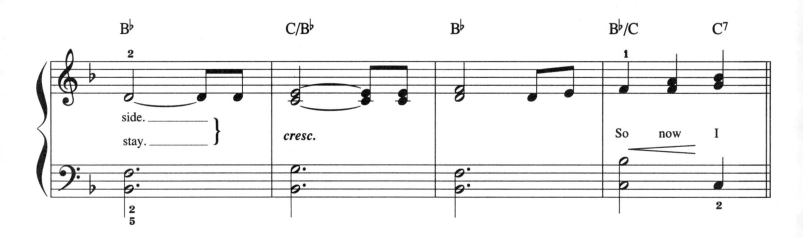

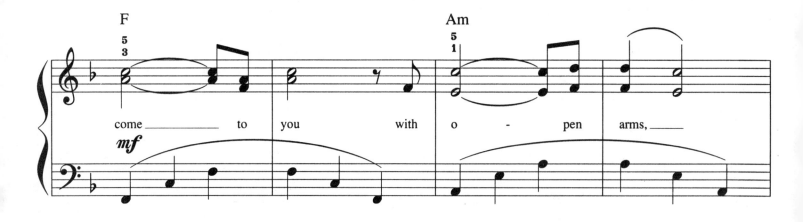

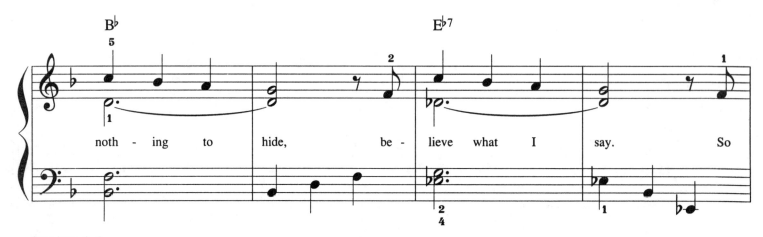

here _____ I am with o - pen arms, _____

hop - ing to see what your love means to me; o - pen

arms. _____

Open Arms - 3 - 3

From the TriStar Pictures Feature Film "ONLY YOU"

ONCE IN A LIFETIME

Words and Music by
WALTER AFANASIEFF, MICHAEL BOLTON
and DIANE WARREN
Arranged by DAN COATES

Some peo-ple fill their lives with emp-ty nights and days that slip a-
Some peo-ple live their lives in com-pro-mise and hide their dreams a-

way. Some search till the end of time, but nev-er find the o-pen arms of
way. Some nev-er take the chance with-in their hands to claim the prize they

fate. One mo-ment comes a-long, and some-one hands your
make. When faith is all you need to hold the hand of

Once in a Lifetime - 4 - 1

To Coda ⊕

SOMEBODY'S CRYING

Words and Music by
CHRIS ISAAK
Arranged by DAN COATES

Verse 3:
Give me a sign and let me know we're through,
If you don't love me like I love you.
But if you cry at night the way I do,
I'll know that somebody's lyin'.

THE SWEETEST DAYS

Words and Music by
WENDY WALDMAN, JON LIND
and PHIL GALDSTON
Arranged by DAN COATES

TAKE A BOW

Words and Music by
MADONNA CICCONE and BABYFACE
Arranged by DAN COATES

Take a bow,___ the night is o - ver, this mas - que - rade___ is

Make them laugh,___ it comes so eas - y when you get to the part ___ where you're

YOU GOT IT

Words and Music by
ROY ORBISON, TOM PETTY
and JEFF LYNNE
Arranged by DAN COATES

Moderately slow ♩ = 88

legato

mp

Ev - 'ry time I look in - to your love - ly
Ev - 'ry time I hold you, I be - gin to un - der -

mp

eyes,
stand.

I see a love that
Ev - 'ry - thing a - bout you

mon - ey just can't
tells me you're my

buy.
man.

cresc.

One
I

118

YOU'LL SEE

Words and Music by
MADONNA CICCONE and
DAVID FOSTER
Arranged by DAN COATES

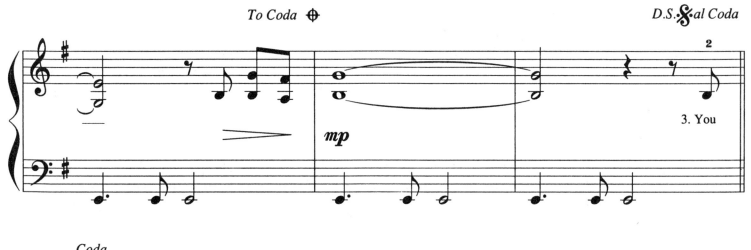

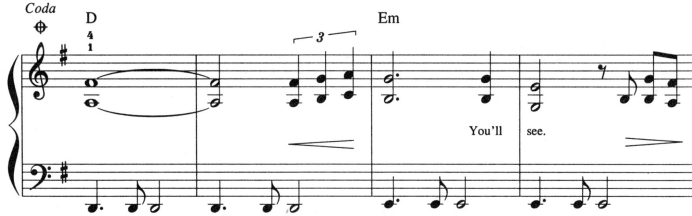

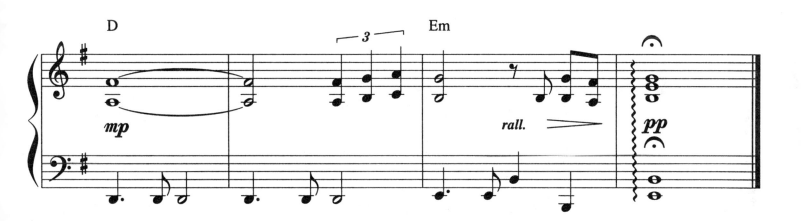

Verse 2:
You think that I can never laugh again,
You'll see.
You think that you've destroyed my faith in love.
You think after all you've done,
I'll never find my way back home.
You'll see, somehow, some day.   *(To Chorus:)*

Verse 3:
You think that you are strong, but you are weak,
You'll see.
It takes more strength to cry, admit defeat.
I have truth on my side,
You only have deceit.
You'll see, somehow, some day.   *(To Chorus:)*

LOVE WILL KEEP US ALIVE

Words and Music by
JIM CAPALDI, PETER VALE
and PAUL CARRACK
Arranged by DAN COATES

Love Will Keep Us Alive - 4 - 1

ANYTIME YOU NEED A FRIEND

Music by
WALTER AFANASIEFF
and MARIAH CAREY
Arranged by DAN COATES

Anytime You Need a Friend - 4 - 1

YOU ARE NOT ALONE

Written and Composed by
R. KELLY
Arranged by DAN COATES